today can take your breath away

today can take your breath away

poems

Marc Swan

Sheila-Na-Gig Editions
Volume 1

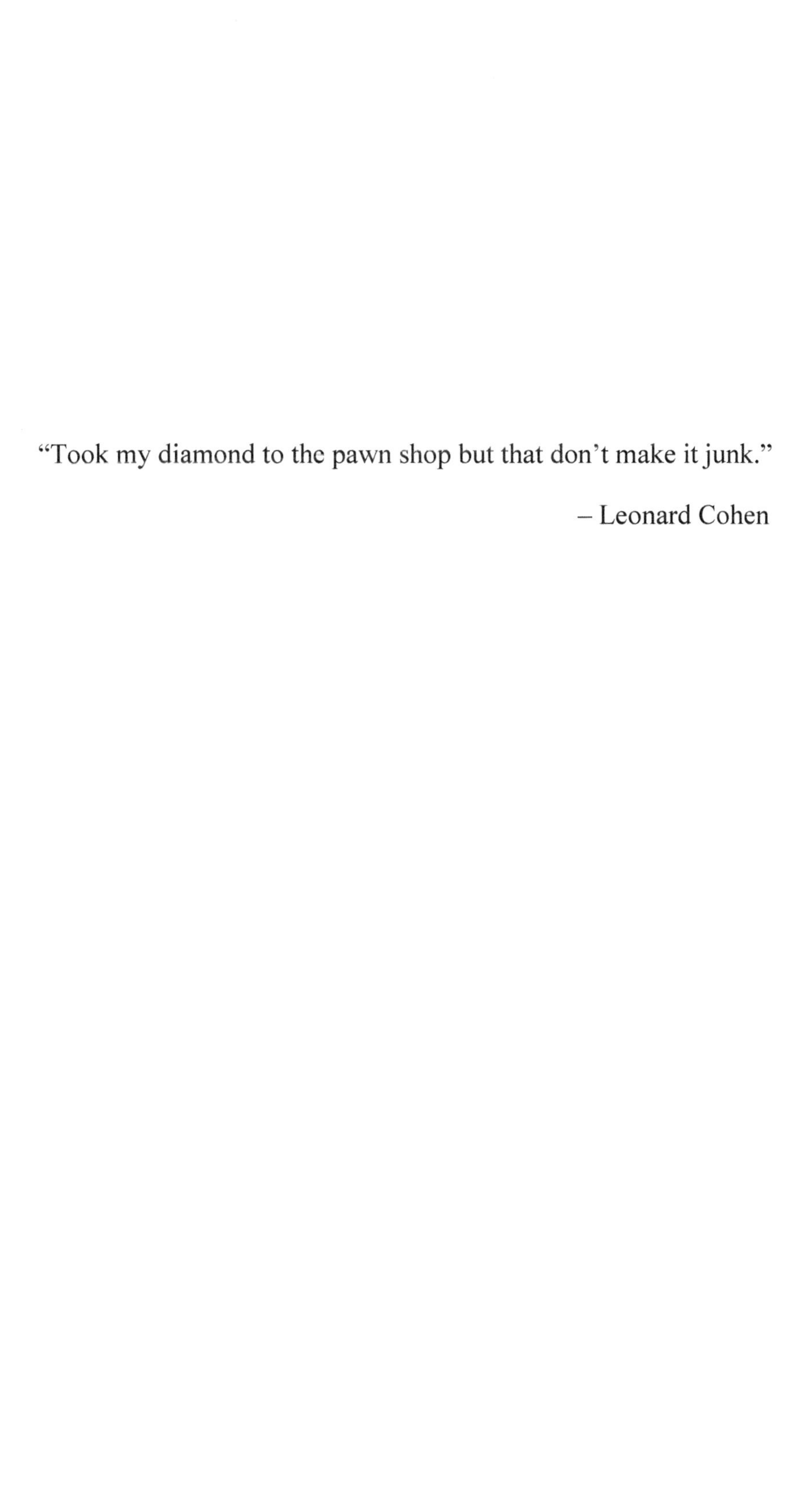

"Took my diamond to the pawn shop but that don't make it junk."

– Leonard Cohen

DEDICATION

For my grandmother, Lillian, who took me to *High Noon*, my first movie, paid the quarter, bought me popcorn, and inspired my lifelong love for film and music, and for Dd who keeps the lights burning when darkness falls.

ACKNOWLEDGMENTS

A heartfelt thanks to the editors and publishers of the following
publications where some of these poems, or earlier versions, first
appeared:

Chiron Review: "3430 Kallaher Street, Memphis, Tennessee"
Clover: "New Year's Day 2017," "Three Wise Men, No Camels"
Coal City Review: "Twenty-five yards away," "When the flame
        flickers"
Concho River Review: "After Life"
Flight Writing: "After the traffic jam"
Mojave River Review: "On the deck, harbor below"
Mudfish: "Before social media"
New Verse News: "January 13, 2017"
Poetry NZ: "On the road to euthanasia"
Poetry Quarterly: "The chill is on"
Ropes: "Hang up"
Scrivener Creative Review: "On a Snowy February Night
        after the Texas Phone Call"
Sheila-Na-Gig online: "Hide and Seek," "Freedom," "Appetite"
The Antigonish Review: "In a Peer Group of French-speaking Africans
        in Downtown Portland, Maine"
The Broadkill Review: "Silver Lake"
The Chaffin Journal: "After hearing Tinariwen's new release,"
        "Creature Comfort," "Citrus Health & Rehabilitation Center,
        Inverness, Florida, 1996"
The Nashwaak Review: "Perspective," "When night falls and wine
        pours"
Westerly: "Karner Blue Butterfly"
West Texas Literary Review: "The Happy Baker, 520 King Street,
        Fredericton, December 2016"

CONTENTS

When the wind blows

There's a sentinel in the treetop—
snow falling, wings steady as branches
shudder, cold wind blowing. We're home
after lunch in a local Asian restaurant
with the dark-eyed server, hair pinned up
into two round nubs like the reindeer look
of Finnish girls in summertime, except
she's not blonde, blue-eyed. She's on break
from her studies in Denmark with fifty
international students *of many colors* she
says. Her color, may be caramel as compared
to the pasty winter white of my wife and me
and our peripatetic friend from New Jersey.
The server smiles when we say we're glad
she's studying journalism—*young involved
inquisitive thinkers are much needed in this
world today.* Then it's just the three of us.
Conversation moves from family matters
to TV series, books, movies, landing
on politics—what we all seem to be talking
about these days. A busboy pours water
as my wife comments on another "asshole"
in the cabinet. He laughs as he pours three
more tables—it's the way it is. People aren't
ready to toss in the towel, say *let's be open
to what this new administration may bring.*
It's family, friends, neighbors gathering
together sharing conversation, good food
and drink, speaking truth not lies.

In a Peer Group of French-speaking Africans in Downtown Portland, Maine

They come together by car, by bus, some walk
to meet each Tuesday in a small room
with many windows and many stories.
They have much to say
and it's so difficult in this new language.
I have come today to talk about listening.
They want to know more about how Americans
think, what they expect, how they move
as easily as they do from one place to another.
Listening is important, I tell them, *understanding
is even more important.* Germaine, a highly
educated man from the DRC, talks of eye
contact and perception. How a friend believes
she lost her welfare benefits
for herself and her four children because
she didn't look the service provider in the eye.
That may or may not be true. What *is* true
is in their culture lack of eye contact
is respectful, eye contact confrontational.
I talk of the fine line between maintaining
one's culture and functioning in a new society.
The six women and five men listen
as the translator takes my words into their words.
There is only the sound of my voice, the translator,
the patter of rain on the many windows.
Their eyes look down, around
searching for the truth they want to understand.

November 22, 2016

Before we finish steaming bowls of homemade
chicken soup at our favorite café on Washington Ave,
talk shifts from his medical concerns
to the dilemma with his wife's family
to the election—all those second guesses
we want to make
to somehow make it different
then we settle on where we were
fifty-three years ago today.
He was in a fourth grade class in Memphis
when the principal released them,
no explanation he can recall.
On the ride home the driver had a transistor radio on.
She slowed to a stop, turned to the students,
eyes red-rimmed, cheeks flushed,
told them what had happened in Dallas
not that far away.
When he got home the house was quiet.
He can't recall if his parents ever talked of JFK.
I was on a Greyhound east of Chicago
on a cold rainy ride through open countryside
when a lady a few rows back turned her radio up high.
We all heard the news.
Two bluesmen began singing "Jesus is Coming Soon,"
one strummed a battered old Gibson out of tune.
A bottle of Southern Comfort made its way up the aisle.
I took a long pull, slipped it to the lady beside me.
She never looked up, just downed a gulp
and passed it along.
The driver stopped. We stood along the road,
a light rain falling—
          I never imagined what the future could hold.

You keep me hangin' on

Why don't you get out of my life
And let me make a brand-new start? – Vanilla Fudge 1967

A song in my head spins round and round
when I read headlines, hear the news,
no TV—that's too much. We're in a time
of change people say. I look out my window,
watch circling gulls drop out of the sky
then up again. Crows sit on rooftops cawing
at gulls, at humans struggling below.

Today I stop at a center helping refugees
and asylees create a new life in a new land,
forced here by events far beyond
their control, their former world shattered
by our bombers, our military might. A local
news team wants comments on yet another
executive order—halting immigration
from seven Muslim countries. An older man,
an immigrant with permanent status,

says he will speak, others in the room are
terrified they'll be seen on TV. Fear like
ice coats the windows, the doors. The older
man, a doctor from Syria, born in Somalia,
talks of a bombing in Mogadishu,
body count, injured, dead. He says if America
helped his country defeat terrorists, the people
would not come here. They would feel safe.
He came here four years ago to escape fear,
repression, to be safe— then it changed.

New Year's Day 2017

I'm at Willard Beach for my morning walk,
sun a spectacular presence on this second day
after the nor'easter, wind calm, a few waves
glimmering off the shore, tide flowing out as dogs
begin to arrive—singles, pairs, a trio of English
bulldogs. The owners slip off the leashes, let 'em
run. You can sense the taste of freedom in the air.
On the far end of the beach before the steep steps
to the hilltop, the three fishing shacks, the view
of Two Lights down the coast, I meet a woman
with one of those little black and white dogs.
We chat about the day, the year, what lies ahead,
the uncertainties in this time we now live. "I never
imagined," I say. She smiles, tells me some of her
story. She just moved back from Savannah after
fourteen years, twelve years prior she lived off
Marginal Way on the industrial side of town.
She's pleasant, a bit rough, but that's understood:
this isn't a social event, just two people passing
time on a holiday morning. I ask about Savannah.
It's on my to-visit list; the red state is a concern.
She isn't a red person she assures me. She talks
about the summers, high humidity, cost of living.
For a while she was on the system, and now
works part time at Starbucks for insurance.
She's an artist and a collector she says, showing
me a piece of split jagged stone with a thin crust
of quartz along the rim. There isn't a lot more.
She calls Cricket, that little dog to her side, gives
him a small treat and they walk down the beach
as I climb those icy steps onto the narrow stretch
that leads to the fishing shacks and a view that
on a day like today can take your breath away.

January 13, 2017

In a short hop against convention, my wife
and I were married on a Friday the 13th. Today
a road trip to honor one. We drive to Belfast, two
hours north, to the Farmer's Market. My wife's
a fan of fresh produce even in wintertime. We
meet a local farmer with twenty-three water buffalo.
I'm staggered by the number, more shocked by how
they survive. This isn't India or Southeast Asia. She
assures me they have a warm barn, plenty to eat.
My wife buys milk for yogurt. The farmer tells us,
you'll be amazed. I'm starting to feel the healthy
pull of the day. We travel Route One to Rockland
for lunch, the warmth of an Irish café. Good food,
friendly staff generous with their time, tables fill
as people trundle in from the cold wind blowing
outside. From here we drive south to Wiscasset
to see a favorite shop owner who in short order
expresses her growing feelings about the election.
Every Friday thru the holidays she's been donating
twenty percent of her sales to five nonprofits that
will likely be battered under the new regime.
Her heart sings Cohen's "Hallelujah" as we talk
of support for those things that separate thinking
folks from those who think chaos should reign.
Across the street in another store, a saleslady we've
never met senses our liberal lean. Running her hands
thru her thick blond-tinted hair, she talks of the march
in Washington and how important it is to be there—
she will "next Saturday." Eyes water as she goes
on about the rip and tear of what was once understood
as democracy too quickly becoming something
with another name from lessons never learned:
fascist, authoritarian, despotic and in these
difficult times we live, simply wrong.

Table Talk, February 15, 2017

First the setting—
heavy rain falling onto the last
fallen snow, wind blowing, car lights
bouncing in yellow rings off windowpanes,
table set for lightly seared bluefin, fresh
green salad with homemade Japanese
dressing, a bottle of Cuvée Bastien,
Eva Cassidy on the CD player.

Talk starts out easy—
about the day, children, grandchildren,
upcoming events: ballet, ice skating, sixth
grade concert—then words darken: a Pakistani
judge ruled Valentine's Day illegal, not sure
where to go with that, on to the latest missteps
of the executive office, followed by tomorrow
night's call for immigrants and human rights
advocates to protest an alt-right speaker
at the local university.

Free speech clangs—
a giant bell in my head. I agree,
we should be open to hearing disparate
views no matter how wrong they may seem
even after four intensely unbalanced weeks.
Civil discourse might enlighten those who
fail to care or fully comprehend. A bumper
sticker on a black pickup pops into my head,
an outline of our country with the words
"Fuck off, we're full." I ask my wife
what time tomorrow do we go?

Perspective

They walk together, five maybe six abreast
down a mile and a quarter stretch of Congress—
ten thousand strong: families, friends, a cross
section of Mainers coming together. I'm struck
by the diversity: older folks with that *I've been
here before and I'm not going away* look, men
in faded jeans, women in brightly colored tees
with slogans, some humor, most about strength,
power, unity, an array of pink pussy hats visible
everywhere. Many hold signs, so many signs,
so much to say. Young families wheel strollers.
Other children walk alongside with signs, happy
to be part of something they have yet to understand,
but they will. Yes, they will. There are
women of color, trans women, women
like my wife who walks with women in hijabs,
friends, along this path that has become a march
with a rhythm. The chant rings loud and clear:

> "What does democracy look like?"
> "This is what democracy looks like."

On the way home, after speeches, crowd alive
with hope and strength for what lies ahead,
one of my wife's friends is confronted by an
angry white man: "Why don't you go home?"
"I am home," she says and walks on.

Three Wise Men, No Camels

At first, the stream is older couples
and single women and men making their way
down the aisles to find seats with friends,
followed by students, many New Mainers—
Sudanese, Somali, Congolese, Iraqis.
A few of the girls wear hijabs, abayas;
the boys in jeans and tee-shirts sit
in the back of the room. Two mics
are set up in front of a podium and four chairs
on a low well-lighted stage, a forum to promote
interreligious dialogue in a time of conflict.
A PBS moderator is there to ask hard questions
of three religious scholars. After a relentless hour
of heady introductions by long-winded community leaders,
the Catholic bishop in pressed priest garb, pot belly
hanging low over creased dark pants, speaks first
in a long halting dogmatic diatribe, saying little
about the subject matter, much
about his academic field
followed by the rabbi, in a nicely fitted suit,
button-down collar shirt, salt and pepper beard.
He has more appeal, a progressive reformed Jew,
open-minded and ready to embrace change.
The third speaker wears thick glasses,
a dark suit and when seated, an austere look.
When he rises to the podium his smile
is broad, embracing. "I'm known as the feminist Imam."
The crowd explodes, people clap loudly.
No music or birds, but you can imagine them flying
around the room flapping and cackling and whistling
a happy tune. He talks of equality in all aspects of life—
religion not for one gender or one denomination,
but the means to create collaboration
where believers and nonbelievers serve others,
build community, practice action. His reach is far,
wide, and full of hope. The rabbi and bishop
sit quietly, eyes downcast, fingers tapping
chair arms, filled, I imagine, with their own hope
that they will not be called on to respond.

Hang up

After fresh green beans, olive oil, pinch of salt,
pan-fried haddock, autumn squash soup with lime,
cilantro, talk shifts from buying the house on Bailey's
Island to today's news—what we do when we settle in
after a day of doing mostly predictable things. I pour
a small amount of cabernet from Washington State.
She has a taste, nods, we move to the world. The world
gone astray. Today in a suburb of Aleppo, a place where
many live, no one dares to go, they dropped barrel bombs
filled with chlorine. Sounds antiseptic and in a way it is.
It cleans the insides of a human breathing apparatus, rips
into the good parts and devours the rest. There are photos
of children with masks, children bent over coughing, blood
spewing. It's an unpleasant experience. There are many
unpleasant experiences each day we live in this world
removed from civility to that other place where
chaos, destruction, pain, and suffering are a way of life.
Recently the news reported a possible "missed call"
from a galaxy far beyond our reach. I imagine
extraterrestrials looking down at a planet mired in fear,
searching for trust. It may be too much. Click.

Karner Blue Butterfly

It's a small show in a grand old
brick synagogue converted to artist
studios—a photographer
hosts a woman's exhibit
of eight beautifully rendered
montages of the Nabokov butterfly.
Endangered blue the artist calls it.
The intricate drawings
detail history, dimension,
environment, the birth and death
cycle of this small
member of the animal kingdom.
I ask of the process,
the lengthy research needed
to understand and create
these heady illustrations. Holding
a glass of Yellowtail chardonnay,
the artist smiles and begins
to tell her story. First
she asks if I'm a Nabokov fan.
I've never had that thought.
Not really, I say, *but I'm someone
interested in learning.*
She walks and talks from one print
to another linking the components
so precisely created. She tells me
of the history of the discovery,
quoting words Nabokov spoke
to describe this delicate species,
of the fires burned in certain
habitats to create ash
for the lupine to flourish—the staple
of the blue butterfly. She tells me
there are only a few places they thrive.
I'm drowning in an academic pool.
I find a convenient segue
and bid her a very nice *adieu*. On the way
out I speak with the photographer.
He tells me of his latest project—

Auschwitz. I'm ready to sink even
lower into an abyss when he explains
the photos are of trees. Trees born
of the dust and dirt of that place.
Trees bent, twisted with a tortured look,
he says, *and that is enough.*

Impact

The planes fly straight and true,
buildings crumble and fall.
Two thousand miles away
a man herding his flock
on a Colorado mountaintop
stops dead in his tracks—
the noise has stopped.
Every morning he wakes up,
every night he drops off
to the boom and snarl of jets
thirty thousand feet overhead.
On this day, the light is bright,
air crisp with early fall,
aspens quake in an easy wind,
birds sing and sheep baa.

Creature Comfort

In the palm of my left hand I hold
this small perfectly formed
creature. Pale brown
on the head and chest
fades to soft
gray on the wings,
pale yellow belly,
tail gray with a lemon
yellow tip, a rakish mask
surrounds the eyes.
With my right forefinger,
I rub the soft
feathers of the underbelly—
the warmth surprises me.
I look into the round dark eyes
glazed over with the last memory,
perhaps, of hitting a window
on a third-story deck.
I cover the body in soft white cloth
to carry down three flights
to the garden
where I find a secluded patch
of unmarked soil
beneath the lilacs
warmed by afternoon sun.
I take my trowel, dig a small hole
where I lay this loosely wrapped
bundle. I spread the freshly
drawn earth
over the now cool body
as thoughts of flight
move me to look upward
searching for the crows
that covet this garden,
creating a solace as natural as light.

On the deck, harbor below

Gulls squawk, balls dribble, hoops clang,
children scream, The Cat sits by the dock
with dead engines, our departure date delayed.
Earlier today, in the bookstore on Congress Square,
the white-haired lady dressed in purple, red plastic
eyeglasses, a warm smile, deep-set brown eyes,
talks with me about poetry. She likes Billy Collins,
the simplicity that takes on new meaning as you read
through the words with a nugget waiting to emerge.
I tell her about Ray Carver, though in the telling
she doesn't hear, not that she isn't listening intently,
but the words are lost to her. She tries to read my lips
and works on her responses, but it's easy to see
she doesn't hear me. Later, from my deck, harbor below,
The Cat patiently sits, waiting, we're all waiting
for something these days, something good to happen,
too much hot air moving our hearts and minds
elsewhere. I think of that woman, ears no longer
attuned to the rhythm and flow of gulls, children,
the playfulness we've lost from long ago.

3430 Kallaher Street, Memphis, Tennessee

The grandmother has no teeth
inside her broad smile.
Her hair is thinning—
Radiation and chemo.
We find out a lot in our ten-minute visit.
She tells us her daughter
and the disabled husband
live here with three young daughters
each with a different father.
She found the body of the first father
murdered in the master bedroom.
Thankfully her daughter wasn't home.
She says she thought we were here
to report the dog.
She asks if we want to come inside.
The space is small.
Dark curtains hide natural light.
There's a makeshift kitchen with a rusty
stove and a sink full of unwashed dishes.
There's a windowless bathroom
with a broken shower rod
next to the master bedroom.
This confounds the grandmother,
*Why would there be a bathroom so far
away from the children?*
Faraway holds in my head—
this is the same small house my wife's
grandmother lived in
when my wife was four.
There was no pit bull chained
to the tree in the yard.
There was no toilet hanging limply
by twisted bolts in the hallway.
There was a flower bed beautifully tended
and the backyard had a tire
swinging free from the magnolia.

Murray Corner

On the curve coming out of the dip where the hawk lies
twisted and torn, I see the first plant belching off to the left
then another and another. A blue haze floats over the coast,
the scent of smoke and cooked fish fills the air. I zig and zag
on the narrow two-lane, a solitary vehicle on a November
morning heading down the Acadian coast. Highway 955 curves
right and straightens dead ahead to Murray Corner, gas station
and general store on the left at the junction of a nondescript road.
In the distance the Confederation Bridge rises eight miles over
Northumberland Strait. Inside an eighty something with granny
glasses, heavy knit sweater guards the cash register. Sitting
across from her three men in flannel and Carhartt nurse coffee,
wooden folding chairs in a half circle as if a pot-bellied stove
glowed in front of them, not the white-haired lady looking stern.
"Bathroom?" "Thru the blue door, down two steps, to the right,
switch on the left." A few minutes later, "Coffee?" She waves
toward a nearby counter with a pot, sugar, "cream in the cooler."
A more pleasant conversation than it sounds; she almost smiles.
The boys are loving the interaction, breaks up the monotony
of another late fall day when life is boarded up for the season,
wood cribs overflow, last load of laundry hanging on the line.

Dropping in at the annual festival

It's a wooden-wheel hearse I realize
behind three women of an earlier time
on guitar and the young fiddle player on the rise
in the rear of the historic museum
on a rainy day in Malpeque PEI,
fresh oysters waiting to be shucked,
mussels steaming in stainless steel pots,
wind easy, rain falling straight down
on the gathered
mostly locals with a few from other provinces
and here we are, the two of us, in this country that draws
us like flies to the honey pot,
searching for the escape from what holds,
the glue of familiarity,
the tethering to known,
locals are open, accepting, and when I tell the older woman
next to the "little neck" shucker that is what we call them
not quahogs; she listens, smiles and says,
"just quahogs up here."

Freedom

When we arrive a fluffy brown cat
dives out the front window of a red Golf.
The lady with the garden hose,
tee shirt, short-shorts, bright green Nikes,
long auburn hair tied back
offers us a beer,
gives a tour of the property.
She's maybe forty,
a Canadian,
college grad living in a wooded glen above a lake
with two cats,
a fresh supply of Heinekens
and a vision of living off the grid.
You're already there my dear
and it's clear that's where you belong.
She's well traveled, a teacher of special needs kids,
looking for that next path to nirvana.
She seems solid in a hip sort of way.
Later in town we hear she's the ex
of the local bluesman—pedal steel no less.
For the past five years
he jammed most Friday and Saturday nights
at The Red Herring,
now an alcoholic on the road searching
for his own brand of enlightenment.
In another era they would've been called hippies,
in this setting maybe eccentric. A crow lands
on a nearby branch, shifts around,
shits directly on the ground—
his back to me, a solitary audience,
unafraid, in charge of whatever the day brings.
Four takes, one word, easy to remember.

Angel on her shoulder
for Alice

Thirty years of confusion, uncertainty,
ups way high,
downs extreme the other way
and today
in the bar by the Bay
where she pours drinks for a local crowd
she tells me about her workouts—
getting stronger physically, mentally,
losing pounds she's carried far too long,
the weight of her young life
becoming unburdened by activity.
When she gets lazy, she says, she thinks
of the angel on one shoulder, devil
on the other. The devil tells her
you don't have to do that;
it's too hard, kick back, light up
another one, just relax. As he talks,
she puts on her workout clothes,
never looks back.

On a Snowy February Night after the Texas Phone Call
for Dd

The table's cleared, board set up,
first letter chosen. Before
the seven letters are drawn,
she sits across from me
still lost in thought.
Her mother is not doing well—
her mother who seldom
had a kind word for her,
who made pig-headed
seem like a normal attribute,
who promised her a house
that never came through—
and she is confused.
The brothers are nearby,
taking care of mother day-to-day
while we live fifteen hundred
miles away. "Not far enough,"
she says. We begin to play.
She's back with me.
First word is *enigma*,
last word *fun*.

After Life

At first it seems simple—
an eighty-seven-year-old woman
in a nursing home
has passed quietly in the night,
no sign of suffering or foul play.
Recently, she'd given a caregiver a check
for ten thousand dollars,
a point of uncertainty in the family.
Words were said,
the secret held—
no consequences for the caregiver
just praise for all the things she did those many days.
After the body is cremated and the documents
begin their orderly float,
a trail of money to the caregiver—
each month a tidy sum paid for all the little things
that were done—
building building building.
The two brothers and sister talk,
spouses in the background,
about the will, securities, belongings,
jewelry, the orphan pet
piddling and shitting.
Finally conversation lands on the caregiver
her brother is a drug dealer,
he lives in a ghetto,
they have no fear of loss.
When the subject shifts to elder abuse,
fear like a vacuum sucks air out of light.
One brother says, "They have hotlines for that."
If someone calls.

Barreling Down the Celestial Highway

It's the shitting blood that stirs the cauldron,
slow decline of twenty-five years has accelerated
we hear in a late night choked-up phone call
and the prospects are looking grim. Next morning
over coffee, my wife talks of good memories—
the times he took care of her when no one else did.
For over two decades she thought every visit
would be the last. That afternoon after a half-bottle
of wine, she calls him unsure of what to say. His wife
said they just look the other way. That rankles
my wife who tries to live a life of transparency.
In that call she tells him of a friend diagnosed
with pancreatic cancer, checking out on his terms.
Talk quickly shifts to his dogs, family updates,
the weather. "Feels like a last call," she says.
Four days later at six am, his eyes roll back in his head,
within hours he's dead. Twenty-five years of slipping
and sliding: quadruple by-pass, defibrillator, tumblers
of vodka by ten am, necrotic colon, perforated
stomach, sepsis after years of living on the edge—
drag racing funny cars with his son, cruising his Harley
in full regalia, banging off rounds with his AR-15,
off-road bikes, ATVs, a cross-country mobile home trip
when he could barely bend his knees—tumbling down
the rabbit hole, shitting blood, wearing Depends.
In the end, his wife of fifty-four years holds his hand.
"I love you," she says. "Do you love me?" This hard-
living man squeezes her hand again and again.

slap ya mama

After the deck is watered down,
eight rental tables, forty-five chairs set up,
grill and boiler dragged out,
guests start to arrive—
family, at first, helping with final prep
then sixty people from his former job,
his wife's former job
with a mix of old and new friends.
His kids and grandkids hold court
pounding Miller and Bud Lites.
One son-in-law has a bottomless
go cup of vodka. It feels like
we made a wrong turn
for a good reason ending up
in Trump country—
a gathering of *good old boys* with Harleys
sporting brightly colored tee-shirts,
hats with bar names
and logos, jeans, scuffed cowboy boots,
their ladies in similar gear
to celebrate the life of one of their own.
Talk shifts from praise for another sunny day
in Houston to 175 pounds of crawfish
being hosed down in giant coolers,
boiled up with potatoes, peppers, mushrooms
spiced with a giant tub of Zatarain's Crab
and Shrimp Boil served with a large dollop
of *slap ya mama* Cajun spices
to pump it up
on to bikes, beer, liquor drinks, weekend
trips to the lake for a waterside
version of the never-ending party.
I think of the electorate—
how the election went the way it went.
After twelve hours and six coolers
of iced down beer, bourbon, and vodka drinks
clarity emerges from the haze.
It's not about who they voted for
or what he stands for

or how many he's shoving out the door.
It's about *change* they say
as they pop another top,
pour another shot.

When night falls and wine pours

Family, for some a litany of memories, for me
an opportunity to explore things never spoken
of when I was a child. I'm in San Clemente. The rains
have stopped, ocean finally calm, sky that deep blue
that only happens in Southern California in wintertime.
My cousin is pouring me one more glass of fine wine,
a high end pinot noir from Sonoma County. We've been
nonstop talking, first at dinner with the four of us, now
five hours later just the two of us looking back on the life
we've lived seven decades from where it all began
in an upstate New York town where two rivers merge
into a mighty flow headed south. We talk of the family
members we barely knew and those we thought we knew
and the way time shapes what is real into what could have
been or might be true. He pours more wine. I hear wind
smacking the shutters, maybe another storm or just nature
having its way, then conversation shifts to his father,
his mother who both had dementia in one form or another
as if there were a format for that kind of loss. His eyes
take on a faraway look, then back to his glass, to me
and he says, "I'm not sure how this will turn out,
but I guess I'm as ready as I could ever be."

After Midnight

Friday night in March, wind calm, waves lazy off the coast,
        we're visiting old friends in Ventura
talking of life, death, spaces in between. We've had dinner,

two bottles of wine—a decent Napa cab and a clean crisp
        Sonoma white. Topic swings to parents,
mostly dead. The wife tells of how her mother, father in their eighties

planned the easy way out: stockpiled pills, wrote to the press,
        to their attorney, called the children
about their last wish to leave on their terms. Next morning

her father called. The pills had expired. They were both
        alive, very tired. A year later she died.
In his nineties, he's alone in a home prattling on to an empty bed.

It's just a dream

I tell myself when she tells me
I'm in the kitchen, she's in the living room
rolling around on her exercise ball
reading the *Portland Herald* on her AirBook
when she looks up at me and exclaims:
"Your forehead is bright red! Let me see it closer."
When I go over to her I collapse in her arms.
She wants to call 911, but can't reach her phone,
in fact doesn't know where her phone is, not
a new thing in her life.
She doesn't feel right laying me down
to find her phone, but adds, "You're already dead."
Dead as a doornail. I'm not smelly dead
like rotted flesh, just not breathing, not pulsing,
not fluttering my eyes or blowing snot
out of my nose or farting—
a bad habit, I know, but when you age the body central
doesn't always comply nicely with what enters it.
"What does it mean?" she asks. Wish fulfillment—
probably not, we work well together. Anxiety over
her new yoga class projected onto a once living
now dream-dead loved one. Maybe. Or just a dream
of loss encompassing those who recently passed—
brother, mother, and all those thoughts over all
those years congealing—the mind, sacred as it may
be, getting just a tad ornery and spiteful.

In an instant

the world I understand, take for granted
becomes another place in my head.
I've pedaled ten miles on my exercise bike,
watched countless gulls fly by,
slipped off
into the daily routine:
making the bed, taking a shower, cleaning up
the kitchen. My wife comes home from yoga,
goes in the bedroom to change.
I grab a tissue to blow my nose.
The next thing I know, Paul,
the EMT, is asking my name. My wife says
later I ask everyone I see
over and over again,
"What happened?" "Did I fall?"
Yes, I've fallen,
dropped like a sack of rocks
to the hardwood floor, splattered
like a watermelon, fresh and ripe;
eyes open, blood pools around
my head. My wife tells me
she thought I was dead.
I'm not dead, just damaged.
The two-flight stretcher ride is bumpy.
Paul is sorry. The next thing I know
I'm in critical care hooked to an EKG,
IV for pain, trying to follow words
from Bridget, the nurse, who says
"Syncope—your words will return." I feel
calmness from above, realize it's my wife
stroking my head, helping me rise from the fog.
It's a long day in ER. When the cloud disperses,
an inch and a half gash
on the back of my head is stapled shut.
Yes, from a special staple gun,
four zaps. I'm released to go home
with caution, they say,
much caution for many days.

Twenty-five yards away

Winter coming on—Great Smokies
loom on the horizon, the last fall leaves
flash red and gold, sun bright, we're in Murphy
at the small A-frame where my parents retired.
On the second day my father says, "Time to sight
in the Remington. Deer season's almost here."
Last time I held a gun I was almost twelve.
On the hillside the woodchuck I shot thrashed
in bloody grass before he blasted it in the head
with his Colt .45. I handed him the rifle. We never
hunted again or did much of anything. On this day
we take the Remington, a box of ammo, a new
target down the slope to a grassy area with a clear
view to a cluster of maples, set up the target
then back to a log about twenty-five yards away.
He hands me the rifle. As I squint thru the scope
he talks of recoil then places protectors over
my ears. I squint again. The target grows clear.
I touch off a round then another and another. I can
sense his excitement as he watches thru binoculars.
I set the rifle down. We move quickly thru knee-high
grass to the target. A fairly tight grouping—a couple
in or touching the bullseye, none far off. "Not bad,"
he says. I haven't felt this close to him in almost
three decades. This was thirty years ago. In 1996,
when he passes, my sister's ex takes the guns.
He's dead now, too. That *thirty-ought-six* is out
there somewhere. If I had it I'd bang off a few
rounds to keep that day crisp in my head.

On the road to euthanasia

When thunder rumbles over his bed
he doesn't move. Does he hear it?
Does he understand? He's been
in this place three years. His pale
watery blue eyes grown accustomed
to changing light of morning, afternoon
and night. He speaks less, mostly phrases,
jumbled thoughts, sometimes a pinhole
appears and words flow. I watch his eyes
flutter. What *does* he hear? His impassivity
is unsettling. He has an untreated angio-
sarcoma, raw and oozing on his forehead,
unclipped fingernails, toenails thick
and gnarly, a shock of unruly white hair.
We wash it once a week, says the stocky
woman with yellow teeth, a crooked smile.
In the afternoon residents gather in the main
room for games and cookies. *His girlfriend,*
my mother says, pointing to a dark-haired
middle-aged woman in a blue hospital gown
staring at the red exit sign over the door.
Her husband comes daily as my mother
does. They never seem to notice, off by
themselves in another time. I think
of choice, the timing of that choice.
When the whippoorwill sings, there'll be
a new day. If you hear it. If you understand.

Citrus Health & Rehabilitation Center,
Inverness, Florida, 1996

On a dreary night in 1991 when I called him in Florida
from Cape Cod and he thought I was the *gas man*, I knew
the threads were unraveling. *Eccentric* my mother, my sister,
his sister, his brother said, but the cards were dealt. I knew
which way the pot was going. The trips over the next few
years were uneventful on the outside, but I sensed change
seeping into his daily routine—missed cues, small jokes
to make it all seem better. In the spring of 1995 as I sat
in the living area of the singlewide, he began tossing
a pillow at me then at my mother, harder and harder. I told
him to stop. The next day they came for him in a white van,
dressed in normal clothes. We told him a special trip had
been planned, kind of an early birthday present. He smiled
remembering that his birthday was a month away.
On my last visit, he was curled on his side, withdrawn,
unkempt, words inarticulate. I spoke with the staff about
his meds. I spoke with his physician about his meds and his
care. Some changes were made. I'm not sure what or when.
I was fifteen hundred miles away. In the end he fell getting
out of bed reaching for glasses that were no longer there,
shattered his hip, stopped eating. When my mother finally
told me what had happened, I missed his passing by
seven hours fourteen minutes. Nurses said he lasted
two weeks before he never breathed again.

Tree of Life

There's a corner of my brain where fear resides,
maybe the size of a grape, but I can feel it pulsing
like a curling wave, swashing in and out. I'm not
sure when I first felt it, maybe when I turned sixty
or sixty-five it started to hum then gained more voice,
building with each annual physical and blood report—
possibilities of those dead relatives speaking to me.
Some easily discounted: my maternal grandmother
and uncle's kidney disease. They died young. I'm not
young. My maternal grandfather with heart disease,
the doc says my ticker ticks perfectly. My paternal
grandfather with stomach cancer, maybe; my mother,
arthritic, died of a deep-seated sepsis from an injury,
not likely. Let's linger a moment on my father—
Alzheimer's and prostate cancer. Every Sunday I work
the Jumble; every day I write these little poems, letters,
keep lists in the right order, pay my bills, remember
the day, month, year, my phone number, address, so far
looks good, but the PSA, that's a different story. Year
by year gaining a point, it directly influences that little
grape in my head that's becoming a kumquat. I think
of the apricot, the orange, and, of course, the apple.

Words, forms, and signatures

In the crowded room that smells of hand sanitizer, soiled
sheets with twin beds side by side, narrow table surrounded
by four plastic chairs, the young nurse in a brightly colored

blouse with Charlie Brown characters on it holds a brochure
with photos of food items. She explains to the Somali wife
which foods have "too many carbohydrates." The wife nods

and smiles. When the nurse leaves, the wife calls her daughter—
"what is kar bo hi drit." An older nurse comes in for discharge
review. Mohamud has been in America many years, knows

much of our language and lifestyle but there are many things
he doesn't understand. The nurse is loud as if her elevated tone
is an interpreter. There's no interpreter. There's no advocate—

only words, forms, and signatures. The nurse drones on and on
as Mohamud and his wife nod, smile. "Any questions?"
Mohamud looks at me, at my wife. We are friends who've

come to give him a ride home after quadruple bypass surgery,
after one week in the hospital. He has done well the nurse says,
there'll be no rehab; he has to leave. "Insurance won't pay."

My wife, a human service worker, does a fast boil. Her concerns
are safety and healing. She talks of the steps into the house,
steps in the house, the children, and food he will eat. "Do you feel

safe going home?" she asks. "No," he says "Write that down."
The nurse nods. My wife presses her. She repeats what she's already
said. Her voice rises as she gathers up the release papers.

"This is beyond my pay grade." She storms out to get the physician
assistant, another woman in one of those Charlie Brown tops
who talks of protocol, policies—"yes, but. . ." On the ride home,

after we help Mohamud up the stairs into his house with ten children,
one a newborn, TV blaring, we say the words that will become
a letter that if nothing else will raise hackles in the cardiac wing.

On a Sunday Evening in June 2017

I've been invited to a feast.
First the sun must set in 24 minutes they say.
For now we are in a small room
on a side street below the area of worship
seated on folding chairs, women on one side,
men seated or standing on the other.
A beatific woman, small of stature,
skin the color of roasted chestnuts,
facial features smooth, warm dark eyes bright
beneath her *hijab* as she smiles, tells me
while I wait I can eat dates. "Three dates,"
she says, "and a *samposa* if you'd like."
The imam says when it is dusk the men
will go upstairs to pray. I'm not Muslim.
I'm a guest, but I'm asked to accompany the men
at the right time. Shoes in hand, I enter the mosque,
set them down behind the door,
walk to a row of chairs along the back wall
of this brightly lighted room.
There are colorful rugs on the floor,
small squares to designate position.
The men file in and line up.
Three other non-Muslim men sit beside me.
The imam speaks to the wall facing east—
yes, that is why—and the ritual takes its course:
standing, bending, dropping into a kneeling position,
buttocks high, head bent low, and up again,
repeated in the order they follow five times each day.
One young man in a long flowing robe uses an *adayge*,
a teeth-cleaning stick, between postures.
Lips move silently as the imam guides the gathered.
Once prayers are said we pick up our shoes, go back
to that small room where food has been laid out.
The non-Muslim women have eaten.
The Muslim women wait patiently holding paper plates
while the men ladle out rice, chicken, sausage, pastries, fruit.
I sit with a man who last ate at 3 am.
"Not a problem," he says, "it's our way of expressing faith—
only one month in a year of life."

Getting to Know You

Our friend invites us to a luncheon for prospective renters
in a retirement community. The waterfront restaurant

is very popular with a more retiring crowd, so that part
seems right. Her cane clicks along the entranceway

as we reach the stairs leading to the upper floor, no elevator.
A white-haired man in his late eighties rides the stair glider

to the next landing and then one more to the dining area.
We mount the stairs aware of our friend's difficulty making

the climb. It's a large room with bright light off the water
cascading through thick pane glass. Tables are set with white

tablecloths, water already poured. First the drink order,
a balding man at our table orders a Bloody Mary, the guy

across from him a gin and tonic, *no fruit*, his wife a mimosa.
It's starting to feel like a party. The hosts grab the mic

to let us know the food and *non-alcoholic drinks* are on them.
Ordering doesn't slow. This crowd knows what they like

and won't take a no. The host couple are opera singers now
renting elder space. They crank up the sound machine, launch

into "God Bless America," *sing along*, and most of the crowd
do, voices building into a patriotic crescendo. Our friend,

a staunch Democrat like us, feels the room tilt further right
than she would like. The next song is "Getting to Know You,"

Their voices are good; choices leave me wanting another glass
of white wine. Music stops, pitch begins, lobster rolls and fries,

more drinks. In the wrap-up they ask if *our guests* would like
one more song, a request lost in the milling of the crowd

moving gingerly toward those two perilous flights going down.

Hide and Seek

My father-in-law was a runner. The story was
he ran with Jesse Owens in the '36 Olympics. I did
a Google search, no results. He may have had
some fame in his homeland. Finns love
their sports figures. It's been a long time. I remember
a good man in a bad situation. Early in life
he married a difficult woman, had two children,
built houses for a living, built his house
on a cul-de-sac curved into the flow of the street.
Masterful when you think about it. His problem
was drink. His wife sloshed scotch, chastised him
constantly for drinking too much beer. I never
heard him raise his voice, hit a child, beat the dog.
It seems he needed a different life, didn't know
how to find it. In the garage workshop where he spent
most of his free time was a laundry basket.
If you dug deep into soiled clothing you'd find
empty Stroh's bottles, lingering drops
dripping on a blouse, towel, his wife's underwear.
Imagine his constant state of disrepair, not thinking
of the *finding*, mostly focused on the *hiding*.
I recently watched a TV series called *Carnivàle*.
In opening credits there's a scene from the '36 Olympics.
I swear the lean Scandinavian looking guy
elbowing in on Jesse at breakneck
speed is my father-in-law with nothing to hide.

The chill is on

as I walk along the shore.
I've entered the *Drug Free Safe Zone*
the sign says.
I look for treasures hidden in crevices,
between small stones,
in the seaweed,
within the detritus of ebb and flow.
No sodden roaches
or syringes in search of an arm.
A smooth round stone catches my eye.
I reach down
          then resist.
The waves are restless,
tide working its way into a late morning crescendo.
I spot a heart stone—
a small gift for her,
then the *Hot Wheels*
laying sideways between dark pebbles.
A Dodge Charger, I think,
tires lost to the sea,
body faded to gray,
a hemi-head fashioned on the hood—
the remnants we carry.

When the flame flickers

It's not a 3 am wake-up call. It's a touch in with a friend
having some medical issues, a friend I've banked a boatload
of memories with over the past thirty-five years, a good friend.
He's a continent and an ocean ride away and I'm in my east
coast condo catching up on what's new and good in his life. He
talks about his wife, her busy life, his son who is off to college.
The conversation flows along and then shifts, at what point
I don't recall. The talk moves to places and times that have held:
fun times, often alcohol and drug induced, all great memories
nonetheless, and people we knew who've passed on, had lived
the good life. It's a grand journey reliving what once fueled
the fire. Conversation wanes. I sense his tiredness. He wants
to keep going; I know he can't. The rush ends as quickly as
it began. This call is different from other calls; I end with
the words, "Love you man, I really do."

Appetite
for Alex

You get the diagnosis, not words you want to hear,
but truth based on all those tests, those conversations
beating holes in the fabric of your mind. This time
there are choices, so you think about it. Then you think
about timeframe, hours strapped to an IV, pain, suffering,
hair loss, not so much, but appetite, food choices. You think
of those things you love to eat and drink and how many
more days you can eat or drink those things: red wine most
of the time, rosé or chardonnay on those hot summer nights,
salads with fresh fruits and greens, St. Agur blue cheese,
and indulgences—potato chips and onion dip, occasionally,
guacamole and those blue corn chips you've grown fond of,
and desserts, not regular fare, but a mile-high banana cream
pie can get you somewhere. You look at the calendar, count
the days, maybe weeks, think of time moving thru space
faster than a dervish whirling in the wind. Do the lights
in the kitchen stay on? Or maybe there's another way.

The Happy Baker, 520 King Street, Fredericton, December 2016

"It's not a patisserie.
It's a bakery," she says.
Her thick black hair pulled back,
low-cut green top sets off a glimpse
of cleavage below a blood-red tinted
stone encased in gold, and a smile
that reaches over the counter to me,
to the woman beside me, to the delivery
man pushing a two-wheeler in the aisle.
I point to a tray of cookies. "That one,"
I say. "An orphan," she says, "created
by the union of cranberries and oatmeal."
Her deadpan humor intrigues me. I order
one and ask her favorite. She doesn't
blink. "Why all of them," she says.
Her hips are slim, eyes bright, full
of mischief. It's been a long time
this feeling coming home.

Silver Lake

Near the high-end furnishings store
next to the building where the ethnic market
stood before the robbery thirty-five years ago
and a brutal event changed the lives
of the older Asian couple who sold
the store and moved to the San Juan Islands,
there's a coffee shop with six dollar cups
of coffee, breakfast plates for fifteen dollars
and a gathering of hipsters chatting, iPhones
in hand or nearby, sharing modern life
on a sunny day in LA. I'm seated at a small table
on the sidewalk with my wife, my good friend
and for an instant, maybe longer, I'm back
in the small white clapboard house with the lemon
tree, lime tree on Duane Street down the hill
from Apex where life had an easy, predictable flow,
every day filled with possibilities of the best kind
until a nine-year-old came into that store; her brain
splattered against the storefront glass
clicked the switch to a time of locked windows
and doors, distrust like an avenging angel
seething into our lives.

Before social media

On that curve heading west on Sunset
past the Roxy an Absolut graphic stands
twelve stories high. In a spring-loaded
moment I travel three time zones, back
seventeen years to the Big Apple, to Caffe
Reggio on MacDougal, to a small table,
a café au lait in front of me, a whipped
cream topped hot chocolate for my ten-
year-old and in walks a news team—fat
cameras, lights. We're chuckling about
the Absolut sign we saw on the side of
a mid-town skyscraper when a bleach
blonde in heels thrusts a mic in my face.
*What does a father think of the Monica
Lewinsky scandal?* she asks. Think. I'm
divorced, seeing my only child on a three-
day weekend. Do I say *I guess he should
have kept it in his pants or maybe pizza
was a bad choice?* What I do say is small
compared to explaining to my daughter
that the things we do in private don't
necessarily stay there, what goes around
comes around, and even the President
of the United States can have a bad day

Signs

No burying my head in sand, but
when I watch news, read headlines
I'm embarrassed to be an American.
I pay taxes, don't text and drive, follow
most of the common sense laws that
under new authoritarian rule appear
to be shifting to uncommon sense. In
that inner sanctum of hope and good
cheer still beating after all these years
I try to focus on the larger world—
what we can do to bring people together
not tear them apart. Simplistic, sure.
Recently I read an article about a town
near Queensland that seems too idyllic
for words—warm weather, ten miles
from the coast, cool shops, organic food,
movies more recent than where I live.
The other day I watched a documentary
on contemporary aboriginal life. This
week it's a binge on *Wentworth* shot
in Melbourne. No kangaroos yet, but
almost daily a duck-billed platypus
rings the bell or strikes the match
illuminating my nighttime head.

After the Traffic Jam

It's almost three—stop and go for two hours
heading south from Portland to Norton, a retirement
party for the creative writing professor who changed
many lives. Road work we realize
as traffic pulses past the first orange construction sign.
When we arrive an hour and a half late
current and former students are gathered in an alcove
in the library, a tub of cold beer, chilled white wine,
snacks on a side table. The honoree sits in the second row,
eyes dead ahead as former students pay tribute, read
poems from now and then, shake the dice on a faraway
time that seems so familiar. My wife steps up to the podium,
poem in hand, words warm and caring as she recalls
how this woman brought light to a time in her life filled
with confusion and, yes, despair. A poem of loss, love,
and a taste of redemption, a nice quality in any poem
Tess Gallagher would say. After the readings, after beer,
wine, snacks, touchback spaces filled with connections
only those who lived it can understand, we head to Wendell's,
a beer pub where memories were shaped for some, for me,
a time to sit with a small cluster of poets speaking the po-talk
that only comes from love of the poetic word.
I'm seated by a flamboyant woman, Japanese-style jacket,
white shirt, blue tie, hair cut short she flips over one ear,
hands in constant motion. "Italian?" I ask.
"Sicilian," she says, "born in blue-collar America."
Earlier this year, on impulse, she traveled to Ireland,
found a publisher for her first book, an eighty-page manuscript
she shares with me. I skim the pages, find myself stopping,
reading, rereading page after page—a solid piece of work
in process for twenty years she says. I wonder at this,
hearing of the acceptance of her poems by magazines far
beyond my reach. The lit world is a remarkable place. We write,
we strive, we find homes for these dog-eared pages we hold onto
revising, revising and on those rare occasions we find
a sense of community when least expected.

Two Steinways in a White Room

A private road leads to a cul-de-sac with a Porsche,
a vintage Mercedes, BMWs, a Lexus or two and now
our well-used Outback parked along the drive of this
pristine seaside home south of Portland. In the alcove,
we chat with a sporty man, thick at the waist, bad teeth,
a Nick Nolte look-alike in a silk shirt, Ralph Lauren
slacks, sandals with no socks; his wife smartly attired
in colorful patterned leggings, form-fitted blouse,
wearing a pair of bright red sandals—a little old
for a trophy, but well maintained for her age. We talk
the idle talk of people in a familiar place meeting people
never before in this place. There will be food, drinks,
heady conversation, but first the recital: ten seniors,
all women except for one baldheaded man with an intense
look. They are dressed in comfortable clothes, though
I sense their uneasiness: tension coats the windows, doors.
I think of our granddaughters' —ten and twelve— never-ending
recitals of various kinds. They move thru their steps with no
fear of loss. If they miss a cue or a chord, they simply move
on. We sit thru seventeen pieces, a few well done. The bald-
headed man, a retired accountant, plays a few solo pieces
with poise, style, a flourish of finger movement. Later we
learn he practices two hours every day, *every day,* he says.
One dark-eyed woman who fretted a lot plays a beautiful
rendition of Piazzolla's *Milonga.* The opening chords
take me to a time when the world seemed to float,
each day chock-full of possibilities.

After hearing Tinariwen's new release

I woke this morning, looked in the mirror,
saw a younger face, tanned, creases smooth,
eyes bright, or at least brighter than last night.
I said words in *tamashek* I didn't know I knew.
I knew many things this brightly lighted morn.
The thing I understood beyond the simpering,
the wailing, the misunderstood was that we'll
survive this time in which we live—a paradox
on values come home to roost like a fast train
to Memphis idling on the tracks. We'll stoke
her up, beat the streets, make the noise, bells
ringing for all the right reasons, peace, our
lantern guiding us into the balmy night.

Specimen

Nine of us seated around a corner table
in a crowded restaurant, small talk enlarges
as the wine pours, lights dim, eight yogis
on their ninth day of yin training finding
commonality as these things often provide
and one spouse, the odd man out until
the next morning when he's center stage.
The "stiff white guy" they observe as
the trainer runs thru a twelve-step series
of relaxation forms, taking the specimen
to another level, an unexpected release
of over thirty years of strung tight energy
flowing from the fascia to the tear ducts.
No one is surprised. Watching, practicing
in pairs, offering sincere concern that
the effort may be too much, but it isn't.

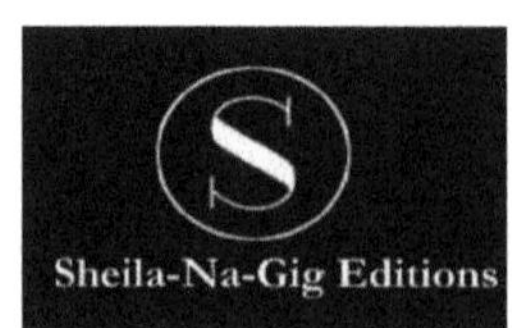
Sheila-Na-Gig Editions